Writing skills

T0370986

This book belongs to

....

Colour the star when
you complete a page.
See how far you've come!

Author: Jon Goulding

How to use this book

- Find a quiet, comfortable place to work, away from distractions.

- This book has been written in a logical order, so start at the first page and work your way through.

- Many of the ideas in the book can be used in all different types of writing.

- Help with reading the instructions and texts where necessary and ensure that your child understands what to do.

- Discuss examples and your child's responses to questions. This will help to deepen their understanding.

- Reassure your child that it is fine to make mistakes.

- Let your child return to their favourite pages once they have been completed. Talk about the activities they enjoyed and what they have learnt.

- Provide plenty of praise and encouragement, not only for doing well, but also for the effort they put in.

Special features of this book

- **Progress chart:** when your child has completed a page, ask them to colour in the relevant star on the first page of the book. This will enable you to keep track of progress through the activities and help to motivate your child.

- **Learning tips:** found at the bottom of every right-hand page, these give you tips and guidance on how you can help your child with the activities and with writing in general.

Published by Collins
An imprint of HarperCollins*Publishers* Ltd
The News Building
1 London Bridge Street
London
SE1 9GF

HarperCollins*Publishers*
Macken House, 39/40 Mayor Street Upper, Dublin 1
D01 C9W8, Ireland

© HarperCollins*Publishers* Ltd 2023
First published 2023

10 9 8 7 6 5 4 3 2 1

ISBN 978-0-00-861791-2

The author asserts the moral right to be identified as the author of this work.

All rights reserved. No part of this publication may be reproduced, stored in a retrieval system, or transmitted, in any form or by any means, electronic, mechanical, photocopying, recording or otherwise, without the prior permission of Collins.

British Library Cataloguing in Publication Data.

A Catalogue record for this publication is available from the British Library.

Author: Jon Goulding
Publisher: Jennifer Hall
Project management and editorial: Chantal Addy
Design and layout: Sarah Duxbury
and Contentra Technologies Ltd
Cover design: Amparo Barrera and Sarah Duxbury
All images: ©Shutterstock.com and
©HarperCollins*Publishers*
Production: Emma Wood
Printed in Great Britain by Martins the Printers

MIX
Paper | Supporting
responsible forestry
FSC™ C007454
www.fsc.org

Contents

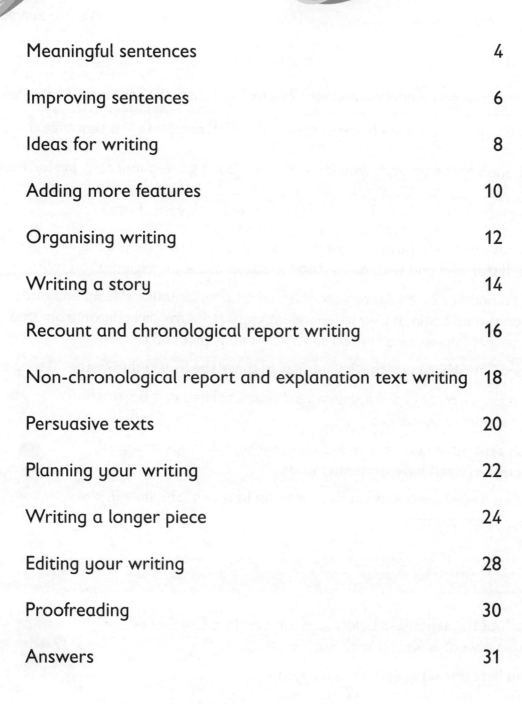

Meaningful sentences

When writing, it is very important that sentences make sense. A sentence must always have an independent clause, which contains a **subject** and a **verb** and represents a complete idea.

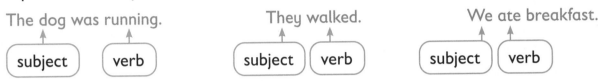

The dog was running.
subject   verb

They walked.
subject   verb

We ate breakfast.
subject   verb

If any parts of an independent clause are missing then the sentence is incomplete.

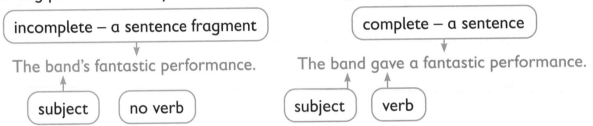

incomplete – a sentence fragment

The band's fantastic performance.
subject   no verb

complete – a sentence

The band gave a fantastic performance.
subject   verb

Sentences must also have the correct punctuation. They should begin with a capital letter and end with a full stop, question mark or exclamation mark.

It can sometimes be tricky to recognise when one sentence should end and another should begin. If two independent clauses follow directly on from one another, it is known as a run-on sentence, and is incorrect.

Valentina Tereshkova was the first woman in space she flew in the Vostock 6 spacecraft.

Each of the two parts are independent clauses. They can be written as two separate sentences.

Run-on sentences can be avoided by ensuring full stops are used correctly between independent clauses.

Valentina Tereshkova was the first woman in space. She flew in the Vostock 6 spacecraft.

1 Each of the sentences below is incorrect. In a few words, explain what is wrong with each one.

The first one has been done for you.

The day was wet and cold .... The full stop is missing.

once, we visited a cave. ....

The long day. ....

They all ran the beach was lovely. ....

2 Change the run-on 'sentences' to separate sentences.

We played in the garden it was a warm day.

_____

She heard the singing it was beautiful.

_____

The players worked hard they won the game.

_____

3 Identify and rewrite the two incorrect sentences below:

The astronauts landed on the moon their mission was going well.

They rested in their craft because the landing had been hard work.

Neil Armstrong stepped onto the lunar surface it was the most famous step in history.

They collected rock samples and completed scientific investigations.

_____

_____

_____

Sentences must be complete. Always check punctuation, and check that sentences make sense with a subject and a verb. It is important to read sentences aloud. Often, if a sentence sounds incorrect or clumsy when said aloud, then it is incorrect.

Improving sentences

Sentences often sound better and are more interesting if more information is added to them.

Use interesting **adjectives** to describe nouns – **magnificent** view, **colossal** ship, **terrible** storm

Use **adverbs** to describe verbs – eating **greedily**, talking **softly**, walking **slowly**

Use **adverbs of time** to describe when the action of the verb is carried out – finally, soon

Use **prepositions** to give an idea of position of things – next to, beneath, above

Use **conjunctions** to join clauses and ideas – and, because, but, or, if, when

Use **pronouns** to avoid too much repetition of nouns – he, she, it, they, we

For example:

The runner stopped. The runner had run out of energy.

adjective	adverb	preposition	conjunction	pronoun

The incredible runner finally stopped next to the road because she had run out of energy.

---

1 Identify the adverb and adjective, then add a preposition to each sentence. The first one has been done for you.

They walked quickly <u>under</u> the magnificent bridge.

       adverb   *adjective*

She lived happily in a house _____ to the sandy beach.

_____ the bed we found a slowly fading old photograph.

I opened the present frantically, desperate to know what was _____ the huge box.

2 Choose a suitable adverb of time from the choices below to add to each sentence to give the reader information about 'when'.

before	soon	often	later

We _____ visit Grandma at the weekend.

They should have looked _____ they crossed the road.

_____ if the ice melted, it would be safe to go outside.

The train would _____ arrive at the station.

3 Complete each sentence by adding a conjunction (from the box below) and a suitable part (clause) after the conjunction. Use each conjunction only once.

Make sure your sentences are punctuated correctly and remember to say them aloud first, to check that they make sense.

if	when	because	and

The huge, luxurious ship needed six restaurants _____

_____

They realised it was an emergency _____

_____

I knew that I would get lost _____

_____

The aquarium has many different fish _____

_____

Encouraging the use of adverbs and prepositions to indicate time and place, and conjunctions to extend sentences and ideas, will allow your child to explore ideas and sentences in more detail. Your child should continue to say sentences aloud but should now also consider where, when and why events take place.

Ideas for writing

Writing is great fun, but it can be tricky to think of **ideas** to write about. One simple way of coming up with an idea is to write about something you know about. This could be a story you have heard or read, a place you have visited, something you have done, or information you have found.

You can think about what you already know, and then find out further information from books, the internet, television and other people.

Writing can be **fiction** which is made-up, or **non-fiction** which is about something real.

1 Draw a line to match each idea below to fiction or non-fiction.

Steam trains helped people travel long distances. They were very popular.

They were approached by a strange creature with eagle's wings and a lion's body.

Fiction

Long ago lived a wizard. She wore a green cloak and a magic hat.

Non-fiction

King Charles III is the first child of Queen Elizabeth II. He has two sons.

2 Think of a story you know. Write three or four sentences explaining what happens in that story. For example:

Goldilocks and the Three Bears

The three bears went out for a walk. Goldilocks went into their house. She ate some porridge, sat on the chairs and fell asleep in baby bear's bed. When the bears returned home, they chased Goldilocks away.

Title of my story: _____

_____

_____

_____

_____

_____

3 Think about something you know about. Draw a picture of what that is, then write two or three sentences about it. Choose a second idea and do the same for that, too.

_____

_____

_____

_____

_____

_____

_____

_____

Discussing ideas with your child can help them to begin to consider and organise sentences before writing. Help them decide whether ideas and sentences make sense before and after they have been written.

Adding more features

Writing is much more than having a good idea and using some great vocabulary. Good writing often includes interesting information for the reader and careful use of language to make the reader want to find out more.

Features such as **fronted adverbials** and **direct speech** can be added to the features discussed on pages 6 and 7 – **adjectives**, **prepositions**, **conjunctions** and **pronouns** – to provide further detail and interest.

A sentence from a story might say: They lured the creature out of the cave.

Other information can be added to the beginning of the sentence as a fronted adverbial phrase to provide further detail to tell the reader more.

Using the food from their packs, they lured the creature out of the cave.

Direct speech can be used to not only tell the reader what characters say to each other but also more information about what the characters are like. It must be punctuated carefully.

"Get the little critter in that bag," growled Jack. ◄── Jack seems angry.

Spoken words and any punctuation that follows are placed between speech marks.

"Don't hurt him Jack. The poor thing is terrified," pleaded Milly. ◄── Milly seems worried about the creature.

---

1 Add a fronted adverbial from the choices below to each sentence.

| **Fearing for her life, Quickly and excitedly, With great care and skill,** |

_____ the artist uses

different brushes and colours.

_____ Grace Darling

launched the boat into the stormy sea.

_____ Jack climbed the

huge beanstalk.

2 Write a sentence using direct speech to indicate the following moods.

Angry:

_____

_____

Happy:

_____

_____

Nervous:

_____

_____

3 Write two sentences that could come from a story you know, and two sentences about something else you know about. Use your own words and try to include at least two examples of fronted adverbials and direct speech.

_____

_____

_____

_____

_____

_____

_____

_____

Discuss how sentence structure can be changed and how fronted adverbials can be added to sentences to provide more detail and interest. Look at how speech is used in stories and how the speech tells the reader more about the character and/or the action.

Organising writing

It is important to be able to use **paragraphs** to group sentences together. The sentences in each paragraph should be linked. They break up the writing into blocks of sentences related to the same idea, which makes it easier to read and understand.

> The train entered through the long, dark tunnel. Everything through the windows was black.
>
> Tilly did not notice. At least at first. Her eyes and thoughts were focused on her book.

> Building the bridge took over six years. Over 400 workers lived onsite by the river.
>
> Once completed, the journey time between the two towns was slashed from over two hours to two minutes.

The first paragraph from the story is about the train going into a tunnel. The second is about a character.

The first paragraph from the information text is about building a bridge. The second is about the benefit of the bridge.

Stories should include an **opening**, **middle** and **end** section (see page 14).

Non-fiction texts usually need:

- an **introduction** (what the text is about) — an introduction to the subject
- **main content** — more detailed information about the subject and why it is important
- a **summary** — a recap of key information
- **subheadings** — used to help the reader to see at a glance what the text is about.

---

1 Draw lines to match the extracts to the three non-fiction text parts below.

> If you ever visit London, be sure to go to the museum, and see all this for yourself. You will not be disappointed.

> The Natural History Museum is in London. It contains exciting exhibits such as dinosaur skeletons.

> The diplodocus is probably the most famous skeleton. The 26m beast now also tours the UK.

introduction	main content	summary

2 Look back at question 3 on page 9 and choose one of the subjects you wrote about. Now write down ideas you might consider including in the following paragraphs:

Introduction:

Main content:

Summary:

3 Write two paragraphs of information using the ideas you have for 'main content' in question 2 above.

Remember that each paragraph should be about a different aspect of your idea.

_____

_____

_____

_____

_____

_____

_____

_____

Discuss paragraphs from a variety of texts with your child. Think about what each paragraph is specifically about and how paragraphs not only differ from those before and after them, but also how they are connected.

Writing a story

Story writing is much more than having a good idea and knowing the story structure. Good writing often includes interesting characters, settings and action which is brought to life through good use of language.

A story is usually divided into at least three main parts:

Opening – introduces characters and where the story is set.

Middle – the main part of the story, full of exciting events.

End – what happens to the characters at the end of the story.

Build-up – events that lead to a problem for the character(s).

Problem – something that the character(s) have to sort out.

Resolution – the events that take place as the character(s) try to solve the problem.

But as you can see above, there are other parts that are often used to link the three main parts of **opening**, **middle** and **end**. The **build-up**, **problem** and **resolution** add more detail and interest.

---

1 Think of a story you know. Write two sentences describing the main character and two sentences describing the setting.

Character:

_____

_____

Setting:

_____

_____

2 Think of another story you know. Add information to the last column below to show how it fits with the story structure.

Opening	**Opening**	Who is the character(s)? Where is the story set?	
	Build-up	What is the character doing and feeling? What is the plan?	
Middle	**Problem**	What problem does the character face?	
	Resolution	How is the problem overcome?	
Ending	**Ending**	How does everything turn out? How does the character feel?	

3 Think about the ending to the story you considered above. Write one or two short paragraphs changing the ending so the story has a different outcome.

_____

_____

_____

_____

_____

_____

Discuss a range of stories and consider how the author describes events and solves problems for the character(s). With your child's own ideas and writing, encourage them to think about how the events link together and how they can describe them.

Recount and chronological report writing

Recounts and **chronological reports** tell the reader what happened during an event. They are both usually written in chronological (time) order, and are written in the past tense.

They are often written in the **first person** using the pronoun 'I'.

As **I** walked down the street, **I** saw a large meteor cross the sky. **I** immediately ran for cover because **I** expected it to come crashing to the ground.

But they can be written in the **third person** using the **pronouns** 'he', 'she', 'they' and 'them'. This kind of writing is common in newspaper reports.

When people saw the fiery rock streak above their heads, **they** immediately ran for cover.

Time is indicated through the use of words such as **first**, **next**, **suddenly**, **eventually**, **meanwhile** and **finally**.

Different times within the recount or report are usually given separate paragraphs. The use of time words and phrases helps the reader to see the connection between these paragraphs.

First, I dived into a shop doorway, but I still felt unsafe. I stood frozen still. **Meanwhile**, I could hear panic all around me. Screams and shouts filled the air.	**Initially**, many sheltered in shop doorways. Fear gripped their bodies. **Suddenly**, there was screaming and panic all around.

1 Below are the first sentences of each paragraph in a recount about a visit to the museum.

Use the following given time words and phrases to complete each sentence.

Eventually	**Next**	**Finally**	**On arrival**

_____ at the museum I headed for the transport exhibition.

_____ I took a look at the town history section.

_____ I arrived at the Space Travel Experience.

_____ as the museum was about to close, I visited the gift shop.

2 Write three sentences recounting something you have recently done. Each sentence should be the first sentence of a paragraph. Remember to use time words and phrases to introduce each paragraph.

_____

_____

_____

_____

_____

_____

3 Read the newspaper report text below and then write two more short paragraphs to continue the story. Remember to use the features of report writing.

Visitors from space

Yesterday, there were incredible scenes in Hyde Park when a strange object landed near the football pitches. It was silver and round, larger than three buses, and had several small windows. People stood and stared with a mixture of astonishment and fear.

_____

_____

_____

_____

_____

_____

_____

_____

Discuss a range of events, giving your child the opportunity to recount them verbally. Encourage the recounts to be a mixture of first person and third person and encourage the use of a variety of time words. Practice writing different recounts, too.

Non-chronological report and explanation texts writing

Not all reports have to be chronological (in time order). Reports that explain about the way things are will include an introduction, a middle (containing all of the information the writer wishes to share) and a summary of the information at the end. Other features include:

- often written in **present tense**, e.g. Squirrels make their nests in trees. They are great climbers.

- **technical vocabulary**, e.g. A squirrel's nest is called a *drey*.

- **subheadings** to make information easier to find, e.g. **What squirrels eat**

The writer must research the subject they are writing about and decide which information to share with the reader.

Key information is given and often expanded on. Sometimes this may be with the use of **parenthesis** such as **brackets** or **dashes**. Examples:

Squirrels live in nests – **known as their drey** – in trees.

Acorns (**the seeds of oak trees**) are a great source of food for squirrels.

---

1 Draw lines to match each subheading on the left to the correct information on the right.

A movie favourite	Fine crystal glasses, exquisite table linen and cutlery, and high-quality chefs await hungry passengers.
Fine dining	The Venice Simplon-Orient-Express is a world-famous luxury train, enjoyed by the rich and famous for nearly 150 years.
Luxurious living	Stories about the train are part of popular culture, and the book and film *Murder on the Orient Express* brought the train to the attention of millions.
A famous train	Private compartments act as sitting rooms by day and beautiful, wood-panelled bedrooms at night.

2 Select the correct information below to use in parenthesis in each given sentence.

> **first conquered in 1953**   **like cats and dogs**   **due to the tides**

The sea level rises and falls (_____)

each day, bringing new creatures to the rock pools.

Mount Everest – _____ – is the

world's highest mountain.

Some types of rabbit can be domesticated

(_____)

and kept as house pets.

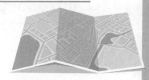

3 Write short paragraphs about where you live.

Use the given subheadings to help you think of ideas. Remember to write in the present tense and to practise using parenthesis for some additional information.

My home

_____

_____

My town

_____

_____

The surrounding area

_____

_____

Encourage the sorting of information into different sections of text using subheadings and paragraphs. Discuss what information each section intends to tell the reader.

Persuasive texts

Writing can be a very powerful tool, not only for entertaining or providing facts, but also for sharing opinions and persuading others about something.

Persuasive texts are written to convince people of a particular point of view. They must be written to make the reader think that this point of view is one they should also share.

Imagine you are trying to persuade people in your town that a new road should not be built because it will damage a local woodland. The reader needs to be drawn in by emotion and facts.

state your own point of view		start to give reasons why

I believe this road should never be built. Ancient trees and rare animal species will be lost forever.

emotion

Do you want to see a beautiful part of our locality destroyed? We can fight against it now.

use **rhetoric** – a question asked for effect	'we' are strong together

The text must be planned carefully with a clear introduction that also states your opinion, several points which give reasons for that opinion, and then a summary of why your opinion is right.

---

1 Draw lines to match the text sections on the left to the ideas on the right.

Introduction	Wildlife will be killed.
	All of the points made show how bad this road will be.
Key point	Trees will be lost.
	I believe that the road should be stopped.
Summary	The road will encourage more cars and pollution.

2 Read each pair of sentences. Place a tick next to the one you think is better for a persuasive text, then write a brief explanation of why.

Lots of trees will be lost. ☐

Many trees, the homes to owls, squirrels and other creatures will be destroyed forever. ☐

_____

_____

Would you like to see this incredible woodland wiped from our amazing local landscape? ☐

A nice, local woodland will disappear. ☐

_____

_____

3 Write two paragraphs persuading your headteacher to let children have longer play times.

You might want to consider arguments such as longer break times increasing health as children run around more, or longer break times giving teachers more time to prepare lessons.

_____

_____

_____

_____

_____

_____

Look at different texts, such as adverts, which aim to persuade the reader to do or buy something. Identify some of the key features and discuss why they are used. You might also listen to and watch TV adverts.

Planning your writing

Before writing any type of text, it is a good idea to make a **plan**. This means considering what the text will be about and how it will be organised.

For a story, consideration will be given to characters, settings and events.

For a non-fiction text, the key information and different sections (possibly using subheadings) will need thinking about.

The planning stage is also a good place to start thinking about some of the **vocabulary** you might use in your writing.

It is always a good idea to write about something you know. For a story, you might base your ideas on a story you know. For non-fiction writing you could choose a subject or idea that you have studied at school, read about or know about from experience.

1. You are going to plan and write a longer piece of text.

In the first instance, jot down (in the space provided below) any ideas you have for the text. This could be a non-fiction piece or a story.

You might like to develop the ideas you used on page 13 or page 15, or think of something completely different, remembering the different types of writing covered in this book.

2 Now, plan your writing below. If you are writing a story, you might choose to use the same format for planning as on page 15. If you are writing a non-fiction text, you might decide to list your subheadings (remembering an introduction at the beginning and a summary at the end) and then note down the key information you will include in each section.

Planning writing will help the writing process stay on track. It frees working memory to allow consideration of finer detail, such as vocabulary and sentence structure, because the general idea for each section of text has already been thought about. Encourage your child to think very carefully about their ideas at the planning stage.

Writing a longer piece

Putting together the different parts of a text to make one whole, longer text is a great skill to practise.

Use your plan from pages 22–23, and look back at the different types of writing and ideas you have practised in this book, before writing your longer text over the next few pages. Use extra paper if you need to.

1 Write your own piece of writing below, using the ideas you have practised with already.

_____

_____

_____

_____

_____

_____

_____

_____

_____

_____

_____

_____

_____

Encourage your child to say sentences aloud before writing them, and to read them aloud to check them once written. This will help them to check that their writing is conveying the correct meaning.

Writing stamina is essential to sustaining ideas and writing longer pieces of text. Your child should be encouraged to use their plan, and to think back to all of the writing skills they know. This exercise can be repeated with different text types.

Editing your writing

Once a text has been written, it is not the end of the process. The next stage is **editing** the writing. This means reading through your work as if you are the intended audience. You need to ask questions such as:

- Does it make sense?
- Could improvements be made to vocabulary, e.g. are the words as interesting and precise as they could be?
- Are sentences as interesting as they could be?
- Is the writing organised well with good use of paragraphs and/or subheadings?

When the text has been edited, read it again to see how well the improvements work.

1 Edit each sentence below by improving the underlined words. Rewrite the text as you edit.

> The R101 was a <u>very big</u> airship. Its first <u>journey</u> was to be from England to India.
>
> This ended in <u>a big problem</u> when the R101 was destroyed in a crash. Forty-eight people <u>lost their lives</u> that October night near Paris.

_____

_____

_____

_____

_____

_____

_____

_____

2 Edit the text below by reading and then rewriting it to make the sentences sound better. Keep the same idea of two children at a beach who want a fish for their supper.

> It was a nice day. Mina and Charlie were at the beach. The sand was nice. The sand was warm. Mina went swimming in the sea. The sea was not too cold. Sammy saw some fish. Mina shouted for Charlie to bring the net. Mina and Charlie wanted to catch a fish. Mina and Charlie wanted to eat fish for supper.

_____

_____

_____

_____

3 Read through your own text from pages 24–27. Now, edit your text. Copy below two sentences that you have changed, and explain why you changed them.

Original sentence: _____

_____

Edited sentence: _____

_____

Reason for changing: _____

_____

Original sentence: _____

_____

Edited sentence: _____

_____

Reason for changing: _____

_____

Proofreading

The final part of the writing process is **proofreading**. This involves checking the text for spelling and punctuation errors. You will have already done some of this during the writing and editing stages, but there may still be some errors. Even the best writers make some mistakes when writing because the mind focuses mainly on the ideas and content being written.

Reading your work aloud can help when trying to spot punctuation errors. Use a dictionary to help check the spelling of any words you are unsure of.

1 Proofread the text below.

Rewrite the whole paragraph, correcting any spelling and punctuation mistakes.

> As the clouds spred across the sky, Adeena's hart quickened Her stomach churned as she wunderd where the others had got to. it was becoming dark and a storm was aproching. Maybe they were on there way but could not see the campsite in the fayling lite. she new she had too do sumthing

_____

_____

_____

_____

_____

2 Proofread the text you have written on pages 24–27. Look carefully for spelling and punctuation mistakes.

Correct these mistakes in your text.

Where possible, early proofreading should be supported with discussion about the mistakes in a text and how they could be changed. If no errors are found, provide your child with further examples of sentences containing spelling and punctuation mistakes to help them get into the habit of proofreading.

Answers

Pages 4–5

1. Missing capital letter on 'once'. Sentence fragment. It is not a complete sentence as there is no verb.
It's a run-on sentence – a full stop is missing after 'ran' and a capital letter is missing on 'the'. (Also accept a suitable conjunction between 'ran' and 'the' such as **and** or **because**.)

2. We played in the garden. It was a warm day.
She heard the singing. It was beautiful.
The players worked hard. They won the game.

3. The astronauts landed on the moon. Their mission was going well.
Neil Armstrong stepped onto the lunar surface. It was the most famous step in history. (Note: a semi-colon could also be used between the two sentence parts but this is not usually taught until Years 5 and 6.)

Pages 6–7

1. adverb – happily; adjective – sandy; preposition – next/near
adverb – slowly; adjective – old; preposition – Under/On/By/Near
adverb – frantically; adjective – huge; preposition – in/inside

2. Examples:
We **often** visit Grandma at the weekend.
They should have looked **before** they crossed the road.
Later, if the ice melted, it would be safe to go outside.
The train would **soon** arrive at the station.

3. Examples:
The huge, luxurious ship needed six restaurants **because** it carried so many passengers.
They realised it was an emergency **when** they saw flames.
I knew that I would get lost **if** I did not take my map with me.
The aquarium has many different fish **and** other sea creatures.

Pages 8–9

1. Steam trains helped people travel long distances. They were very popular. – non-fiction
They were approached by a strange creature with eagle's wings and a lion's body. – fiction
Long ago lived a wizard. She wore a green cloak and a magic hat. – fiction
King Charles III is the first child of Queen Elizabeth II. He has two sons. – non-fiction

2. Answers will vary. Ensure that the given response summarises the chosen story.

3. Answers will vary. Ensure that the sentences make sense and are relevant to the chosen ideas/drawn picture.

Pages 10–11

1. Discuss which responses fit best.
With great care and skill, the artist uses different brushes and colours.
Fearing for her life, Grace Darling launched the boat into the stormy sea.
Quickly and excitedly, Jack climbed the huge beanstalk.

2. Examples:
Angry: "You've made me so cross," snarled his sister.
Happy: "This is just the best news ever!" cried Dad.
Nervous: "I'm not sure I can do it. It's almost impossible," stuttered Jim.

3. Answers will vary. Look for examples of direct speech and fronted adverbials in the sentences written.

Pages 12–13

1. If you ever visit London, be sure to go to the museum, and see all this for yourself. You will not be disappointed. – summary
The Natural History Museum is in London. It contains exciting exhibits such as dinosaur skeletons. – introduction
The diplodocus is probably the most famous skeleton.
The 26m beast now also tours the UK. – main content

2. Answers will vary. Check that ideas fit with the relevant sections.

3. Answers will vary. Check that sentences make sense and that paragraphs are used well.

Pages 14–15

1. Ensure that the sentences are accurate and focus on character and setting.

2. Answers will vary. Ensure that ideas in each section are suitable responses to the questions in the second column.

3. Answers will vary. Check that sentences make sense and that paragraphs are used well.

Pages 16–17

1. **On arrival** at the museum I headed for the transport exhibition.
Next, I took a look at the town history section.
Eventually, I arrived at the Space Travel Experience.
Finally, as the museum was about to close, I visited the gift shop.

2. Answers will vary. Ensure each sentence starts with a time word or phrase.

3. Answers will vary. Ensure the paragraphs are clearly defined and are about different parts of the report.

Pages 18–19

1. A movie favourite – Stories about the train are part of popular culture, and the book and film *Murder on the Orient Express* brought the train to the attention of millions.
Fine dining – Fine crystal glasses, exquisite table linen and cutlery, and high-quality chefs await hungry passengers.
Luxurious living – Private compartments act as sitting rooms by day and beautiful, wood-panelled bedrooms at night.
A famous train – The Venice Simplon-Orient-Express is a world-famous luxury train, enjoyed by the rich and famous for nearly 150 years.

2. The sea level rises and falls **(due to the tides)** each day, bringing new creatures to the rock pools.
Mount Everest – **first conquered in 1953** – is the world's highest mountain.
Some types of rabbit can be domesticated **(like cats and dogs)** and kept as house pets.

3. Answers will vary. Ensure ideas and sentences relate to the given subheadings.

Pages 20–21

1. Introduction – I believe that the road should be stopped.
Key points – Wildlife will be killed.; Trees will be lost.; The road will encourage more cars and pollution.
Summary – All of the points made show how bad this road will be.

2. Many trees, the homes to owls, squirrels and other creatures will be destroyed forever. ✓
This gives more detail making people think about the poor creatures, and more powerful words are used, e.g. *destroyed forever* rather than *lost*
Would you like to see this incredible woodland wiped from our amazing local landscape? ✓
This asks a rhetorical question. It addresses the reader directly and helps them to see that they can play a part.

3. Answers will vary. Discuss the persuasive language used.

Pages 22–23

1. Answers will vary.

2. Answers will vary. Ensure that there is a planned structure and enough key information to allow the writing of a full text from the plan.

Pages 24–27

1. Child's own written text.

Pages 28–29

1. Example vocabulary underlined:
The R101 was a colossal/vast/huge airship. Its first voyage/flight was to be from England to India.
This ended in disaster/catastrophe/tragedy when the R101 was destroyed in a crash. Forty-eight people died/perished that October night near Paris.

2. Example:
It was a beautiful day and Mina and Charlie were at the beach. The sand was soft and warm. Mina went swimming in the sea. It was not too cold. She saw some fish and shouted for Charlie to bring the net. Mina and Charlie wanted to catch a fish so they could eat it for supper.

3. Answers will vary.

Page 30

1. As the clouds **spread** across the sky, Adeena's **heart** quickened. Her stomach churned as she **wondered** where the others had got to. It was becoming dark and a storm was **approaching**. Maybe they were on **their** way but could not see the campsite in the **failing light**. **S**he **knew** she had **to** do **something**.

2. Answers will vary.